# MACHINES ON THE MOVE

# MOTORCYCLES

## James Nixon

amicus

Published by Amicus
P.O. Box 1329
Mankato, MN 56002

Printed in the United States of America, at Corporate Graphics in North Mankato, Minnesota.

Library of Congress Cataloging-in-Publication Data
Nixon, James, 1982-
   Motorcycles / by James Nixon.
      p. cm. – (Machines on the move)
   Includes bibliographical references and index.
   ISBN 978-1-60753-060-2 (library binding)
   1. Motorcycles–Juvenile literature. I. Title.
   TL440.15.N595 2011
   629.227'5–dc22
                                        2010006429

Created by Appleseed Editions Ltd.
Planning and production by Discovery Books Limited
Designed by D.R. ink
Cover design by Blink Media
Edited by James Nixon

Photograph acknowledgements
Alamy Images: pp. 13 top (David Hancock), 17 bottom (Mark Boulton); Baal: p. 29 middle (Oliver Keller &
Tilmann Schlootz); Confederate Motorcycles: p. 28; Corbis: p. 9 bottom (Jack Fields); Getty Images: pp. 8 bottom
(Tim Boyle/Newsmakers), 18 (Bryn Lennon), 27 bottom (Jeff Kowalsky/AFP); Harley-Davidson: p. 9 top; Honda
News: pp. 5 top, 7 top, 11, 13 middle, 13 bottom, 20, 29 bottom; Kawasaki: p. 12; Monotracer.com: p. 29
top (Peraves Ltd, Switzerland/www.monotracer.com); Photolibrary: p. 7 bottom (Corbis); Shutterstock: pp. 4 (Robert
Kelsey), 6 (Ljupco Smokovski), 8 top, 14, 15 top (Bill Lawson), 15 bottom (James Steidl), 17 top, 19 (Tan Kian
Khoon), 21 top, 21 bottom (Marcel Jancovic), 22 (Margo Harrison), 23, 24 top (Andrea Leone), 24 bottom, 25
(Michael Stokes), 26 (Colin Hutchings); Suzuki: p. 5 bottom; Vertika Trykes: p. 27 top (Vertika Trykes-USA, Inc.);
Yamaha: pp. 10, 16.

Front Cover: Shutterstock: top, bottom (Stephen Mcsweeny)

DAD0042
32010

9 8 7 6 5 4 3 2 1

# Contents

What Is a Motorcycle?    4

Motorcycle Controls    6

Classic Motorcycles    8

Superbikes    10

Touring Motorcycles    12

Customized Motorcycles    14

Scooters    16

Track Bikes    18

Dirt Bikes    20

Stunt Riding    22

The Small and Powerful    24

Big Bikes, Trikes, and Quads    26

Motorcycles of the Future    28

Glossary    30

Index and Web Sites    32

# What Is a Motorcycle?

**Motorcycles are two-wheeled motor vehicles. They are ridden by millions of people all over the world.**

There are many different types of motorcycles. They are designed for everyday use, for speed, or for muddy off-road racing. All motorcycles have similar parts.

4

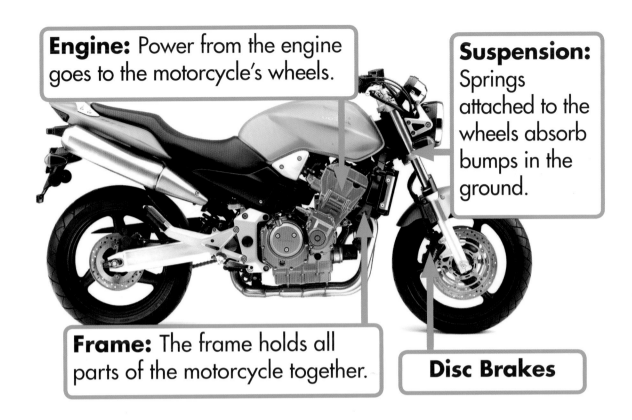

**Engine:** Power from the engine goes to the motorcycle's wheels.

**Suspension:** Springs attached to the wheels absorb bumps in the ground.

**Frame:** The frame holds all parts of the motorcycle together.

**Disc Brakes**

## Fast Cycles

The Suzuki Hayabusa is one the fastest road bikes in the world. This mean machine can go over 200 mph (354 k/h). Its smooth shape cuts through the air at high speeds.

# Motorcycle Controls

Motorcycle riders control their bikes using both hands and both feet. They use controls on the handlebars to increase speed and to control lights. They use a foot pedal to change gears.

**Clutch:** For changing gears

**Gear Change Pedal**

## Gears

The gears change the amount of power going to the motorcycle's wheels. If the bike is going slowly, it needs to be in a low gear. To change gears, the rider pulls in the clutch and moves a pedal with his or her left foot.

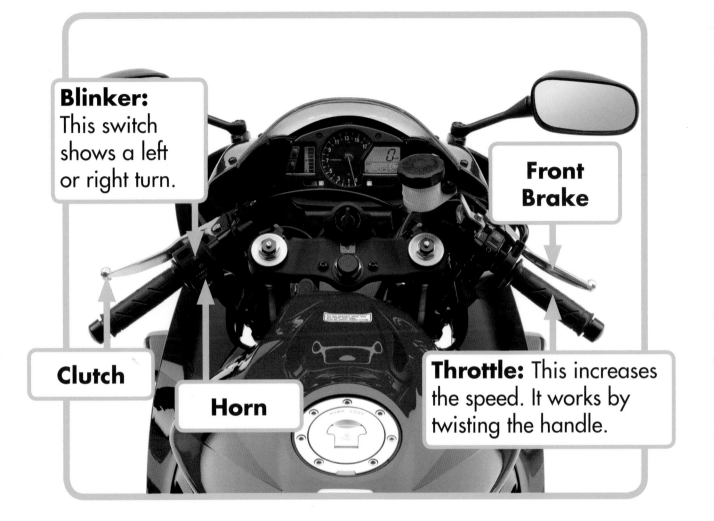

**Blinker:** This switch shows a left or right turn.

**Front Brake**

**Clutch**

**Horn**

**Throttle:** This increases the speed. It works by twisting the handle.

Dials in the middle of the handlebars show how fast the motorcycle is going and how far it has traveled.

## Brakes

The rider presses a brake pedal with the right foot, and pulls a brake lever with the right hand to slow the motorcycle down.

**Rear Brake Pedal**

# Classic Motorcycles

**Motorcycles have been around since the early 1900s. By the 1920s, they had become very popular.**

Popular motorcycle models from the past are collected and ridden by people today. They are known as **classic motorcycles**.

Classic Motorcycle

Some classics are rare and expensive. This bike, made by a company called Indian, was priced in a sale at $58,000.

Harley-Davidson has made motorcycles for over 100 years. Today, they still build motorcycles in the style of the old classics.

## Early Motorcycles

**The first motorcycles looked like ordinary bicycles with an engine bolted to the frame.**

# Superbikes

**Superbikes are the fastest and most powerful bikes on the road. Superbikes have engines as big as a car's engine.**

A superbike's engine rests inside a lightweight frame. Their power and lightness make these bikes fast and furious.

# Engine

A bike engine (right) works like a car's. **Fuel** is burned inside metal blocks called **cylinders**. This makes **pistons** inside the cylinders move up and down. The energy in the moving pistons is changed into a turning movement. This drives the back wheel of the bike.

## Leaning Over

**A motorcycle rider can drive around a corner very quickly by leaning into the bend. Sometimes, they almost touch the ground. If riders lean over too far, they will crash.**

# Touring Motorcycles

**Touring motorcycles are the biggest bikes. They are built for long-distance trips. There is space for two people and their luggage.**

The engine on a touring bike must be powerful. This is because the bike weighs as much as a small car. Touring bikes must also be comfortable. The driver sits up straighter than he or she does on other bikes.

## Sidecars

A sidecar can be bolted onto a touring bike to give room for an extra person and more luggage.

**Heated Handgrips**

**Storage Box**

Touring bikes have everything you need for a long trip. The seats and handgrips are usually heated. There is often extra equipment, such as a radio, CD player, and **satellite navigation** system.

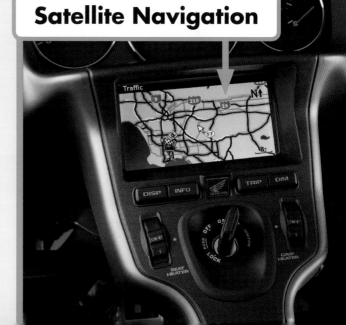

**Satellite Navigation**

# Customized Motorcycles

**Motorcycle owners often change the look of their bikes by adding or removing parts. This is called customizing. Customized bikes often look completely different from any other motorcycle.**

Owners of customized motorcycles want their machines to stand out from the crowd. They may give their bike an awesome paint job.

Some people add power to their bike by putting in a bigger engine. They also make the frames lighter so the bike will be very fast.

**Lightweight Frame**

**Front Forks**

## Choppers

Choppers are custom bikes that have had big changes. They are not easy to ride, but they look cool. The seat is low to the ground, and the front **forks** are really long. The name comes from the fact that parts have been removed, or "chopped" out.

# Scooters

**Scooters are smaller, less powerful motorcycles. They use little fuel and are cheap to run.**

People often drive them for short trips in cities. Scooters can be driven quickly through traffic jams. They are easy to park, too.

# Parts of a Scooter

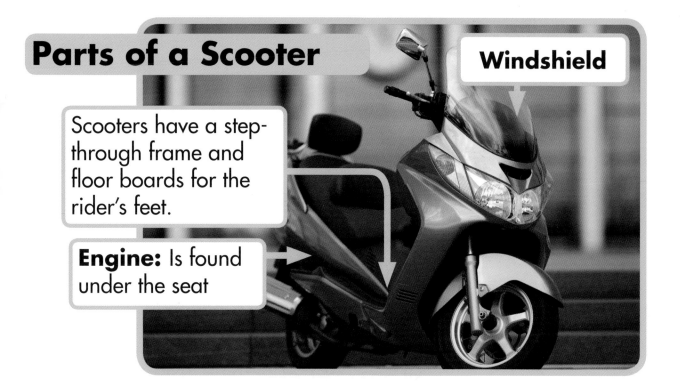

**Windshield**

Scooters have a step-through frame and floor boards for the rider's feet.

**Engine:** Is found under the seat

# Electric Bikes

When motorcycles burn fuel, fumes escape into the air. Electric bikes do not burn fuel, so they are much cleaner. These bikes get their power from an onboard **battery** pack. Under the seat is a recharger. This plugs into an electric outlet, and charges the batteries when they run down.

# Track Bikes

**Racing bikes around tracks is a fast and exciting sport. The fastest races are MotoGP races. The bikes in MotoGP reach speeds of 215 mph (350 k/h).**

The top superbikes on the road are raced in the Superbike World Championship. The Ducati 1098R (below) won the World Championship. One of these bikes can cost $41,000.

## Safety Gear

If a rider crashes, the only protection is his or her clothes. Riders wear a helmet and a thick leather suit. Knee pads protect their knees when they lean into a bend.

Knee Pad

## Tires

Motorcycle tires are rounded. This helps the wheels grip the track when the bike leans into corners. In a race, the rider has a choice of tires. Smooth tires are used when the weather is dry. If the track is wet, grooved tires are used to give better grip.

# Dirt Bikes

Motorcycles that are ridden off-road are called dirt bikes. They are designed to deal with rough and muddy ground.

**Engine:** This is high above the ground to keep it from hitting any bumps.

**Tires:** They are big and knobby to grip the soft ground better.

**Suspension:** A dirt bike's suspension is much more springy than that of a normal motorcycle.

Motocross is a type of dirt bike racing. Riders race around a muddy track, leaping over ramps, dips, and hills.

## No Brakes!

**Speedway is another type of dirt bike racing. Bikes race round a small oval dirt track, but without brakes! The drivers slide the bikes sideways around the bends.**

# Stunt Riding

**Not everyone rides motorcycles in the normal way. Stunt riders use their machines to perform jumps and tricks.**

Motocross racetracks are used as arenas for stunt competitions. A group of judges looks for the rider with the best jumps.

## Trials Bikes

In a trials competition, riders take on a dangerous obstacle course. The aim is to not touch the ground with your feet. Trials bikes are extremely light and have no seat!

## Big Air

Some crazy riders attempt massive jumps on their bikes. In a competition called "Big Air," riders take off of a ramp and do jumps of over 66 feet (20 m)!

# The Small and Powerful

Motorcycles come in all shapes and sizes. Tiny pocket bikes look like toys, but these are serious machines.

Pocket bikes work just like bigger bikes. Children and adults race them around tracks.

## Superstar Biker

Valentino Rossi from Italy is one of the best motorcycle racers of all time. The five-time winner of the MotoGP championship started his career racing pocket bikes.

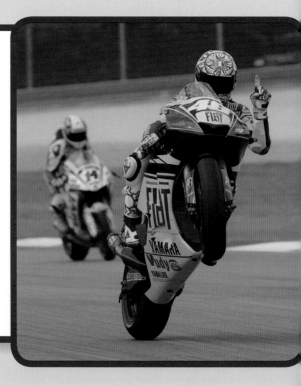

# Drag Racers

Drag racing bikes are the most powerful of all bikes. These machines are designed to go as fast as possible in a straight line. They can get from 0 to 60 mph (100 k/h) in just one second!

The engine on a drag bike is so powerful it can lift the machine right off of the ground. The **wheelie bar** on the back stops this from happening.

Wheelie Bar

# Big Bikes, Trikes, and Quads

**Big motorcycles have many uses. Police forces across the world use them. They are quick and can also carry equipment for most emergencies.**

Ambulance workers use motorcycles in some cities. They can dodge heavy traffic and still carry much of the same equipment as a four-wheeled ambulance.

Trikes are three-wheeled bikes. They are good for long trips. The extra wheel makes the bike more stable and gives the driver more room for luggage.

## Dodge Tomahawk

Quads are four-wheeled motorcycles. The Dodge Tomahawk is an amazing quad, which can travel at over 400 mph (640 k/h). It needs four wheels to handle the power of the huge engine, but it can still lean into corners like a motorcycle. It is not allowed on public roads.

# Motorcycles of the Future

**Motorcycle designs are always changing. What will they look like in the future?**

Motorcycle makers build **concept vehicles** to show off their new ideas. They are first displayed at shows, but could end up for sale in the future.

Designers create some amazing new looks. This "Renevatio" concept bike has all its working parts visible.

The Peraves "Monotracer" has the thrills of a motorcycle, but also has a roof and doors like a car.

The Hyanide has a **track** that could pull the machine through deep mud, sand, and snow.

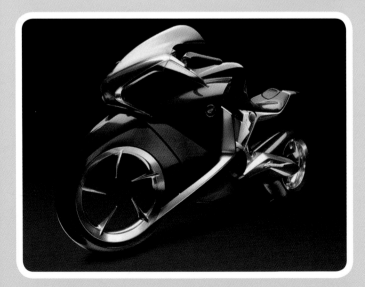

The Honda V4 (left) is a stunning concept bike. Could motorcycles look like this in a few years?

# Glossary

**battery**  a container storing chemicals, which produces electrical power

**classic motorcycles**  the best and most famous motorcycles of the past

**concept vehicle**  a new design of vehicle, built for display at a motor show

**cylinder**  a chamber inside a motorcycle engine, where fuel is burned

**forks**  the supports for the front wheel of a motorcycle

**fuel**  material such as gasoline that is burned in an engine to produce power

**MotoGP**  a championship for the fastest racing bikes in the world

**piston**  a part inside the cylinder of a motorcycle engine, which moves up and down to provide energy to the bike's wheels

**satellite navigation**  a system which receives signals from satellites in space to help vehicle drivers find their way

**superbikes**  the fastest, most powerful motorcycles

**track**  an endless belt that a vehicle's wheels run on for riding on soft and rough ground

**wheelie bar**  stabilizer attached to the back of a drag racing bike to stop the vehicle from flipping into the air

# Index

blinkers 7
brakes 5, 7, 21

choppers 15
classic motorcycles 8–9
concept motorcycles 28
custom motorcycles 14–15

dirt bikes 4, 20–21
drag racing 25

early motorcycles 9
electric bikes 17

frame 5, 10, 15, 17
fuel 11, 16, 17

gears 6

motocross 21, 22
MotoGP 18, 24

pocket bikes 24
police motorcycles 26

quads 27

scooters 16–17
sidecars 13
speedway 21
stunts 22–23
superbikes 10–11, 18
suspension 5, 20

tires 19, 20
touring bikes 12–13
trials bikes 23
trikes 27

## Web Sites

**http://auto.howstuffworks.com/motorcycle.htm**
Find out more about how motorcycles work.

**http://www.motogp.com/**
Official web site for MotoGP.

**http://www.amaproracing.com**
Official site of the American Motorcyclist Association.